Around the House

the

Jane Bidder

FRANKLIN WATTS
LONDON • SYDNEY

First published in 2006 by
Franklin Watts
338 Euston Road
London NW1 3BH

Franklin Watts Australia
Hachette Children's Books
Level 17/207 Kent Street
Sydney NSW 2000

Copyright © Franklin Watts 2006

Series editor: Jennifer Schofield
Designer: Ross George
Picture researcher: Diana Morris

Acknowledgements:
The author would like to thank Marry Bellis
of http://inventors.about.com. for her help
in researching this book.

British Museum/HIP/Topfoto: 22bl. Peter Connolly/AKG Images: 6bl.
Andy Crawford/Watts: 16t, 31.Mary Evans Picture Library: 7.
Randy Faris/Corbis: 10t.Don Geyer/Alamy: 11c. Hutchison/Eye
Ubiquitous: 10b. Museum of American History: 24bl.Picturepoint/
Topham: 16b, 19c, 21bl, 21c. Steve Prezant/Corbis: 24tr. Rayathon: 15.
Science Museum/Science & Society Picture Library: 26bl. Science
Museum Pictorial/Science & Society Picture Library:18bl. Science
Picture Library: 25.Victoria & Albert Museum, London/BAL: front
cover cr,8bl. Gary Vogelmann/Alamy: 6tr. Stephen Welstead/Corbis: 22tr.

A CIP catalogue record for this book
is available from the British Library.

ISBN: 0 7496 6400 2
Dewey Classification: 609

Printed in China

Contents

About inventions

An invention is a device or gadget that is designed and made for the first time. The person who makes the device is called an inventor. In this book, we look at inventions that are found around the house, who invented them and how they have changed over time.

Easy living

Many gadgets have been made because people want to improve their lives. For example, it is much easier to press a switch on a washing machine than to spend hours washing clothes by hand. Not only do inventions like these make our lives easier by saving us time, but they have also changed the way we live.

From one, comes another

Not all inventions are thought of instantly - many of them develop from other inventions and are changed and improved over time. For example, clocks have become more and more accurate timekeepers since the initial breakthrough of using springs and cogs.

You will find timelines throughout this book. They show in date order when a specific breakthrough or invention occurred.

Sometimes the dates are very exact, but other times they point to a particular historical era, for example the Middle Ages.

Use these timelines to keep track of when things happened.

Accidentally invented

Not all new inventions are planned or developed from another invention; sometimes breakthroughs happen by accident. For example, when Dr Percy Spencer was doing research on radar in 1946, he discovered that microwaves cooked food. A year later, the first microwave oven was used in a restaurant.

Toilets

When you are on the toilet, you probably do not think about it as an amazing invention. However, toilets have not always been as hygienic and as comfortable as many are today. Most people had to make do with a hole in the ground.

Friendly chat

Nearly 2000 years ago, the Romans built rows of toilets with a stream of water running beneath them. These toilets were part of public bath houses. People could sit on the toilet and chat to the person sitting on the one next to them.

Potties for adults

During the Middle Ages, wealthy people may have had toilets with water in the bowl, but many families could not afford such luxury. Instead, they sat on large bowls, which looked like toddlers' potties, called chamber pots. These smelly pots had to be emptied after each use.

Modern toilets

The breakthrough came in the late 1800s when Thomas Crapper, a London plumber, invented a new toilet. It had a valve and a U-bend pipe which meant there would always be water in the pipe. This stopped smells from the drains coming back into the house. The toilet also flushed waste away to newly built sewers.

U-bend

TIMELINE

1000 BCE
King Minos of Crete in Greece is the proud owner of possibly the first flushing toilet.

100 CE
The Ancient Romans have toilets in their public baths.

200 CE
A Chinese king is buried in a tomb with a stone toilet in case he needs it in the 'after-life'.

1594
England's Sir John Harrington builds a flushing toilet for Queen Elizabeth I.

1775
Britain's Alexander Cumming patents a flushing device.

Late 1800s
Thomas Crapper invents a toilet with a U-bend.

Keys and locks

Keys and locks help us to feel safe and they keep our valuables secure, but they are definitely not new inventions.

Fancy keys from long ago

About four thousand years ago, the Ancient Egyptians started to make keys and locks out of iron. Some of these had very fancy designs and looked quite pretty.

Keys for noblemen

By the Middle Ages, important people had their family symbols and coats of arms engraved on their keys and locks. Travelling workers, called journeymen, would also make keys for gates, chests and cupboards, as well as doors.

Beating the burglars

In 1851, the American Linus Yale Junior invented the famous Yale lock that is used today. The lock has a main barrel with slots set in a line. There are also two metal pins. The first pin fits closely to the walls of each slot and the second pin is just above the first one. When the key is turned, the second pin is pushed down onto the first by a spring. This aligns the slots and unlocks the lock.

Padlocks
In the early 1920s, German-born Walter Schlage invented a push-button locking device similar to the padlocks that are used today.

Toothbrushes

From when our first teeth appear, we are taught to clean them twice a day with a toothbrush and toothpaste. But did you know that the Ancient Egyptians brushed their teeth, too?

Ancient toothbrushes

Sticks with frayed ends have been found in Ancient Egyptian tombs. Experts think that the Egyptians used them to clean their teeth.

Get flossing!

It is thought that prehistoric humans used very thin twigs and tough stems to floss their teeth.

Animal hair

In the 1400s, the Chinese invented a toothbrush made of wild boar hairs fastened to a bamboo handle. These toothbrushes were adapted in Europe with horse hair for bristles.

Fantastic plastic

In 1937, Wallace H Carothers from America invented a type of plastic called nylon. A year later, nylon was used to make many things, including the bristles found on toothbrushes. Since then, most toothbrushes have been made from plastic.

TIMELINE

3000 BCE
Ancient Egyptians chew on sticks to clean their teeth.

500 BCE
Toothpaste is used in China and India.

1400s
Toothbrushes with bamboo handles and wild boar-hair bristles are made in China.

1938
The first plastic toothbrushes are sold.

1939
The first electric toothbrush is made in Switzerland.

1939–1945
During the Second World War, soldiers are ordered to clean their teeth regularly. The tooth-brushing habit spreads.

Clocks

From the moment we wake up to the sound of the alarm clock, we use clocks to check that we are not late for school, work, trains and buses. But it took a while for people to be able to time their day like clockwork.

Sun clocks

The first clocks were 'Sun clocks' which were built by the Ancient Egyptians in about 3500 BCE. The clocks were tall, four-sided pillars which cast shadows according to the Sun's position. Unfortunately, because they relied on sunlight, the clocks could work only in the daylight hours.

Tick tock!
Clockwork is the way a clock is powered or made to move. This can be by weights pulling down or coiled-up springs slowly unwinding.

Mechanised clocks

In 1656, the Dutchman Christiaan Huygens made the first pendulum clock. Its hands were driven around by the swing of a pendulum. A year later, Huygens made watches which were powered by small wheels and springs.

pendulum

Using crystals

In the 1970s, clocks were introduced that used the energy of quartz crystals to move the hands. When an electrical field runs through the crystal, it vibrates. The vibration causes the clock's regular ticking and accurate timekeeping.

TIMELINE

3500 BCE
The Egyptians build Sun clocks.

300 BCE
Water clocks are used by the Greeks.

700 CE
Water clocks are made into sand clocks.

Middle Ages
Clocks are powered by weights and wheels.

1510
The German Peter Henlein invents the 'spring-powered clock'.

Mid 1600s
Clocks have a hand added to show minutes.

1656
Huygens makes the first pendulum clock.

1950s
Atomic clocks are used.

1970s
Quartz clocks become popular.

Mi-rowav oven

Microwave ovens heat up or cook food much faster than ordinary ovens. Although they are a fairly recent invention, microwave ovens are popular, especially with people who are in a hurry or do not want to spend hours cooking.

Popping mad!

Microwave ovens were invented in 1946 when the American engineer Dr Percy Spencer was heating a glass tube to do research on radar. To his surprise, he discovered that sweets in his pocket, which were near to the tube, melted. That made him wonder whether a tube or a box could be used to heat food. So he put some corn in the tube and it popped!

Giant Radarange

In 1947, the Radarange oven (far right) was made for restaurants to use. It was big compared with the microwave ovens found in today's homes.

TIMELINE

1946
Dr Percy Spencer discovers that sweets in his pocket have melted when he experiments with microwave energy.

1947
In the USA, the first microwave ovens are used by restaurants.

1960s
People begin to use microwaves in their homes.

Today's ovens

At first, many people did not want to use microwave ovens as they feared they would become ill from the microwave energy. But microwave ovens became more popular by the 1960s and, today, many homes and restaurants have them in their kitchens.

More than ovens
Microwave energy is not used just in ovens, it is also used in televisions, telephones, and in machines to catch cars that are speeding.

Light bulbs

It is hard to imagine our homes, schools and cities with no electric lights. However, before 1811, people used candles and lanterns to find their way in the dark.

Before light bulbs

In 1811, England's Sir Humphrey Davy discovered how to pass electricity between two poles to make light. His invention, called arc lighting, was used to

light streets in Europe and the USA. The arc lights did not glow for long and a new invention was needed.

Different strengths
The strength of a light bulb is measured in watts. The higher the wattage, the brighter the light.

The first electric light bulbs

The light bulb as we know it was invented by two Canadians, Henry Woodward and Matthew Evans, in the 1860s. As they did not have enough money to develop their invention, the American Thomas Edison is said to have paid them for the idea and made the first electric bulb in 1879.

How do bulbs work?

Light bulbs use electricity to heat a thin piece of metal wire, called a filament, so that it glows. Edison used carbon for the filament and he sucked as much air as possible out of the bulb so the filament did not burn. Since about 1909 tungsten has been used to make filaments because it does not melt easily.

filament

Vacuum cleaners

Without vacuum cleaners, our homes would be dusty and dirty. These machines use an air pump to suck up dirt from the floor. The dirt is collected in a bag or container and then emptied.

Booth's big machines

H Cecil Booth first came up with the idea for a vacuum cleaner when he put a handkerchief on top of a chair and breathed in through it. When he turned over the handkerchief it was dirty, so he designed 'Booth's cleaning pump' - a huge machine that cleaned floors by sucking up dirt.

On a carpet
About 75 per cent of the dirt on carpets is made up of dead skin. The flakes end up on the floor with hair, mites and other dirt.

Super Hoover

In 1906, America's James Spangler made a vacuum cleaner out of a fan, a box, a pillowcase to catch the dirt, and a rotating brush to sweep the carpet. Two years later, he sold his idea to the Hoover company. The new cleaner sold so well that some people still use the word Hoover instead of vacuum cleaner.

Lighter and powerful

Not many families had a vacuum cleaner before the Second World War because they were still quite expensive. But after 1945, they were mass produced and so became cheaper and more affordable.

1869
The Whirlwind vacuum cleaner goes on sale – but it is not powered by electricity.

1901
The first electrical vacuum cleaner is invented by Britain's H Cecil Booth.

1906
James Spangler makes a smaller, easier-to-use vacuum cleaner.

1908
Spangler sells his idea to the Hoover Company. They launch the first vacuum cleaner to use attachments and a cleaning bag.

1930s
Plastic vacuum cleaners go on sale. They are lighter and easier to use, so more people have them.

Washing machines

Washing machines certainly make our lives easier. Instead of washing our clothes by hand, we are able to have clean clothes at the touch of a button.

Non-electrical machines

The first non-electrical washing machine was invented by Britain's H Sidgier as long ago as 1782. Sidgier's washing machine looked like a cage with wooden rods that were turned by a handle. People put their dirty clothes on the rods and poured water over them.

Talking machines
Washing machines that talk to you are not far away. Perhaps they will say things like 'fill up with detergent' and 'close the door'.

Thundering machines

The first electrical washing machine was made in 1906. It was named the Thor, after the Viking god of Thunder, because it was very noisy. The machine had a small motor but water could spill out onto the wires, giving the person using it an electrical shock.

Twin tubs

During the 1960s, twin tubs were invented. These washing machines had two drums next to each other. Clothes were washed

in one drum and then lifted out and put in the next one to spin them. Today's machines have a single drum that both washes and spins clothes.

TIMELINE

1782
H Sidgier designs the first washing machine. It looks like a cage with rods going into it.

1906
The first electrical washing machine is made.

1937
The first automatic washing machine is made. It costs almost as much as a small car!

1950s
The first washer-dryers are invented. Not only do they clean clothes, but they also tumble dry them.

1960s
Twin tub washing machines are sold.

1970s
Front loading washing machines become popular.

Chairs

We sit on chairs every day. But have you ever wondered who invented the very first chair?

Chair fact
One of the largest chairs ever made was built in America in 1959. The chair was nearly six metres tall.

Egyptian chairs

Chairs were found in the tombs of Egyptian pharoahs (rulers) as long ago as 5000 BCE. The chairs were made of wood and had beautifully carved legs.

Carved chairs

Between 1300 and 1600, chairs became more popular in Europe. Some chairs were elaborately carved. From the 1600s, chairs began to have upholstered seats. The seats were covered in materials like silk and velvet which made them comfortable to sit on.

Shaker chairs

In America in the 1700s, a religious group of people called the Shakers made chairs. Shaker chairs were wooden and had backs made from two or three slats. The designs were simple and had no decorations. Shaker chairs are still popular today.

TIMELINE

5000 BCE
The ancient Greeks and Egyptians have chairs, but not all of them have backs.

Middle Ages
Chairs are a luxury, so many people sit on the ground, on stools or on chests.

1300s onwards
Chairs become more popular. Monks sit on wooden chairs when they are writing.

1600s
Chairs have seats made of soft material.

1700s onwards
Shaker chairs are made in America. Other chairs become more elaborate. They have carvings and upholstery made from beautiful materials.

1900s onwards
Chairs are made from materials such as plastic and metal.

Fridges

Have you ever noticed that if you do not keep certain food, such as cheese, in a fridge it goes bad? Long ago there were no fridges. Food had to be stored in an ice box to keep it cold and fresh.

The first fridge

In 1844 Dr John Gorrie made an ice-making machine. He put water in a container and covered it in brine. He then passed very cold, compressed air through the brine. This chilled the brine, which chilled the water so it froze. The brine remained liquid as it freezes at a lower temperature than pure water.

Ammonia fridges

In 1859, the Frenchman Ferdinand Carre developed Gorrie's ice-making machine further. Instead of using cold air to cool the liquid, he used ammonia gas instead. Ammonia is easier to chill to very low temperatures, so it is an even stronger coolant. Although Carre's machine worked very well, it was too big to be used in homes.

Fridges at home

In 1873, a German called Karl von Linde built a fridge for homes. His design was developed by others and more and more people started buying fridges. By 1918, Frigidaire had become a leading fridge maker and was making different kinds of fridge.

TIMELINE

1300
Someone in China discovered that when salt water evaporated, it took in heat and kept food cool.

1805
Oliver Evans built a basic fridge model.

1844
America's Dr John Gorrie makes an ice-making machine.

1859
Ferdinand Carre uses ammonia gas as a coolant in his fridge.

1918
Frigidaire becomes a popular brand of fridge.

Other inventions

There are many other inventions that are found around the house that are also important to our daily lives.

Ironing boards
America's Sarah Boone invented an ironing board in 1892. Her ironing board was made so that sleeves could be ironed.

Irons
The electric iron was invented in 1882 by America's Henry W Seeley. His 'electric flatiron', as it was called, weighed almost 7 kg and took a long time to warm up. Later in the 1950s irons with wooden handles were made (see left). Today, irons are much lighter and they also warm up almost instantly.

Cutlery

Although forks were used in 600 CE in the Middle East, they were used in Europe only in the 1500s. Spoons were used as long ago as the first century. During the Middle Ages, they became popular, and were made from wood or horn. Before table knives were used, people used their daggers to eat with. Then, in about 1600, special table knives were made from metals such as silver and pewter. Today most cutlery is made from stainless steel.

Plates and bowls

Some of the oldest pottery bowls are believed to have been used in Japan in 10,000 BCE. Today, crockery is still made from pottery but it can be made from glass and plastic, too.

ELECTRICITY

For hundreds of years, there have been many scientists who have worked with electricity. However without Alessandro Volta and Michael Faraday's discoveries, many of the inventions in this book would not be possible.

Italy's Alessandro Volta found that if he dipped a piece of copper and a piece of zinc in salt water, an electrical current was produced. This was the first electrical cell. Volta then made a pile of these cells to make the first battery.

Michael Faraday from England discovered that electricity could make magnets turn in circles. Scientists used this discovery to create electric motors that are found in many household inventions.

Timeline

5000 BCE
Chairs are made in Ancient Greece and Egypt. They can be seen on ancient relics such as vases.

3500 BCE
Sun clocks, the first kind of clock, are invented.

2000 BCE
One of the first keys is used in an Egyptian palace.

1000 BCE
King Minos owns a flushing toilet.

100 CE
The Romans have toilets with water flowing below them.

700 CE
Water clocks are made into sand clocks.

900 CE
English craftsmen make beautiful keys out of metal.

Middle Ages
Keys for homes are made.

1400s
In China, toothbrushes are made with bamboo handles.

1510
A spring powered clock is made by Peter Henlein.

1594
A flushing toilet is built.

1600s
Chairs have seats made of soft material.

1656
Christiaan Huygens makes the first pendulum clock.

1775
Alexander Cunning's design for a flushing toilet is patented.

1782
The first non-electrical washing machine is made.

1811
Arc lighting is invented by Sir Humphrey Davy.

1844
Dr John Gorrie makes an ice-cooling machine.

1851
The Yale lock is invented by Linus Yale Junior.

1859
Ferdinand Carre uses ammonia gas as a coolant in his fridge.

1879
Thomas Edison makes the first light bulb.

1901
A design for the first electrical vacuum cleaner is sold.

1906
The first electric vacuum cleaner is made by the Hoover company.

1939
The first plastic toothbrushes go on sale.

1946
Microwave ovens are invented after sweets melt in a scientist's pocket.

1960s
Twin tub washing machines are sold.

Glossary

Ammonia
A colourless gas that has a strong smell. It has been used as a refrigerant.

Brine
Salty water.

Carbon
A substance that is found in all plants and animals.

Coats of arms
The special patterns or badges that represent a family or country.

Evolved
When something develops or changes to become something else.

Hygienic
Clean and germ-free.

Iron
A hard, silvery grey metal.

Middle Ages
The period in history from about the 10th century until the 15th century.

Monks
Holy men who live in monasteries.

Microwave energy
Power from electricity that heats things very quickly.

Patents
When someone owns the rights to an invention so that it cannot be copied.

Prehistoric
From a time so long ago that things were not written down.

Quartz crystal
A shiny stone formed from the mineral quartz.

Second World War
The war against Germany between 1939 and 1945.

Sewers
A system of pipes that takes away waste from toilets.

Tungsten
A metal that does not melt easily.

Valve
An opening in a pipe that allows water to go in or out of the pipe but not at the same time.

Websites

www.nationalgeographic.com/
features/96/inventions/
Have loads of fun playing games
about inventions.

http://home.howstuffworks.com
Find out how everyday inventions
work by searching for them on this
website.

www.uspto.gov/web/offices/ac/
ahrpa/opa/kids/index.html
Visit the American Patent and
Trademark Office's website to find
out more about inventions and how
they are patented.

www.sciencemuseum.org.uk/
on-line/huygens/page1.asp
Find out more about the invention
of the clock and its inventors such
as Christiaan Huygens.

www.getty.edu/art/collections/
collection_types/w2032823-
1.html
Take a virtual tour of the Getty
Museum and see pictures of all kinds
of chair, including a miniature throne
that dates from 1425 BCE and armchairs
from 1810.

http://invention.smithsonian.org/
centerpieces/edison/
Play a fun game to find out more
about Thomas Edison.

www.yalelock.com/Yale/Templates/
LocalNormal____1630.aspx
See great pictures of old Yale locks and
read about Linus Yale's inventions.

Note to parents:
Every effort has been made by the publishers
to ensure that the websites in this book are
suitable for children, that they are of the
highest educational value, and that they
contain no inappropriate or offensive
material. However, due to the nature of the
Internet, it is impossible to guarantee that
the contents of these sites will not be altered.
We strongly advise that Internet access is
supervised by a responsible adult.

Index